PASSIVE INCOME WITH VENDING MACHINES

Step By Step Guide to Starting Your own Vending

JAMES MOORE

Introduction

Hi, and welcome to my title on vending machines. It's really wonderful to see you here. I'm James Moore, and I'd like to shed some light on business regarding vending machines, so then you can see if this might be a great income idea for you. I truly believe that knowledge is power, and if you gain it from a great source you can move forward more easily, and with added confidence too.

If you're looking for a great avenue in which to earn a steady income, one which operates every day, and continually pays with little supervision or intervention, then I might have the ideal solution for you!

Have you ever thought about entering the office coffee business? Or even the vending machine business? Hmm, it's an unusual idea for most, but that's okay. We'll see if it's up your alley, soon.

I can tell you right now, and from my experience; there's money to be made for both, and there's no need for you to be one of the larger coffee brands or large vending corporations, either. You can begin to scoop up your fair share of office accounts. I know this to be true because I've been doing this for the past years.

While I was busy building my business, I accidentally stumbled into the "office coffee" part of things, and this was when customers began asking if I was in a position to help them out. With this twinkling of an idea, I went home and did quite a bit of research about what they'd asked me, and after some homework and juggling of numbers... I finally made the jump, and I helped my customers out in the process.

They were extremely happy, and I haven't looked back with even one single regret, none at all, actually. Naturally, I'm going to tell you how I think a vending business (which is profitable) needs be run, including all the steps which I took in getting there. A lot of the techniques work for both the coffee brewer scenario and the vending machines, and this is mostly because the overall principle is the same. You are looking at a customer's problems, and then offering a first-class solution to them. It's kinda simple, when you see it like that.

My Vending Business Venture

HOW VENDING STARTED FOR ME

I started this side of my business with one machine, which I bought off a friend for $600 (secondhand). He was moving and offered me the machine which was already located where I worked at the time. My friend showed me how to load the machine and remove the money, as well. He also told me where he bought his products and handed me their contact info. It was like a jackpot for me at the time.

From that point, I was up and running with no idea about what I was really doing. I didn't even know what to do to fix the machine if it broke. After the first couple of weeks, I realized *how* I was making money. I ran over the calculations:

A case of soda $7.00

Machine soda price $1.00

Case of 24 soda sold $24.00

Machine profit $17.00 per case

I was selling 3 cases of soda per week because the weather was warm, and that was a weekly profit of $51.00 ($204.00 per month), and it only took 10 minutes of restocking every time it was running low.

That first machine was paid off in a couple of months, and after that, everything was profit for me to keep.

Not Everything Was Easy

At this point, I was overly excited and motivated, and I realized there was potential to make good money. I had a number in my head, and I began processing all the possible calculations:

If I had 10 machines and I could sell 3 cases of soda from each machine, then I'd have $510.00 profit, per week.

I went out to do more research, and at that time, this meant going to the place where my friend bought his machine. I explained my situation, and I had no idea what I was doing. However, I wanted to find new locations. The guy told me to get out and start knocking on doors, or cold calling. I was not (and still am not) good at sales, and I really had no idea about what to say.

He told me to tell them, "I wish to place a machine in your company location, and I will fill it."

With that, I went knocking on doors, and went from company to company, not knowing what to expect, or what to say! Unfortunately, in business, there are obstacles to overcome. My biggest obstacle was the steady stream of… rejection.

I walked from one place to another and didn't even arm myself with a business card, flyer, or brochure. "No, sorry, we have machines," or "No, not interested. I don't think it'd do well here." This was what I heard time after time, again and again.

It took a lot out of me, and I almost decided to quit the vending side and any thought of expanding this idea, along with it. I needed to learn more about this type of business while I went along.

I stumbled along, and when I could I'd often approach other

vending operators and ask loads of questions. Not that they offered too much information.

After a while, I got a break when a friend told me his mother managed an apartment building, and that I should speak with her. I did, and told her what I was trying to achieve. She let me set up a soda machine and said if I gave an excellent service and donated a couple of cases of soda for their summer barbecue, she wouldn't be asking for a commission.

Commission, I thought? That's something else you'll need to know. There is always someone who wants a piece of your pie. To start, I had no idea people would ask for a commission. I agreed and set up my machine.

The machine did well. The apartments only had 8 floors, but there were over 100 units, and a lot of them were occupied by young people. I sold about 4 cases per week. The machine I placed there, I'd bought from another friend who was also starting in the same business. I paid $1000for the machine. It was a second-hand *Dixie Narco*. I'd advise using *Dixie Narco* because I've found them to be the most reliable. The second one I'd suggest is *Royal Vendors.*

I was shown how to set it up so it could vend a variety of soda (and bottled water too). As a quick note: bottled water costs around 17 cents each. At a price of $1.00 (or more) in your machine, that is where you make your best profit. I felt lucky when my friend's mother referred me to other apartment buildings in the area.

I spoke to all three and made deals with two. For my machine placement, I paid my first commission. In about 2 weeks I had their buildings up and running with *my* soda machines. These complexes had 2 or 3 separate buildings, so I bought 5 used machines from a local dealer. I paid around $1000 for each machine.

I was feeling pretty pleased with myself, and thinking I was on the road to making serious money. It only took a short time to restock each machine and these sold anywhere from 3-4 cases per week, each.

I spent a few thousand dollars to buy these machines, but I wanted to pay them off quickly. Things were going along nicely until a couple of months later, when I got a call from one location. Two of them had been broken into.

I found 2 machines with doors ripped open and empty cash boxes, and as well as this, they stole the coin mechanisms, and these cost me $300 (each) to replace.

Harsh Lessons Learned

I should've taken time and done some research before deciding where to place my machines. I, unfortunately, found this out after the event, and the buildings had a history of thefts from their laundry machines, so I found out.

I should've at least talked to some of the tenants and got some feedback on the buildings. Coffee brewers are very much different, they don't hold money, and they are inside an office. This gives added security and peace of mind.

I came to the conclusion: every outdoor or public location which you place a machine is at risk. I also found that high schools, apartments, and general outdoor areas are the worst for vandalism.

There is potential to make some fantastic sales, but the loss and damage can outweigh these, in an instant. Aside from that, I had no insurance to cover the costs, so I needed to pay cash for the repairs. Now you know, always have some insurance for your own protection. I can't stress this enough.

Although I began with the coffee brewers, that isn't the full story, really, because the other side of my business is an extension of that, and I broadened my horizons into vending machines. I already had the techniques for scouting locations, and for how to approach people, and so it seemed like a logical step. This was mostly because I didn't need to learn much that was new. It was a "business evolution" rather than a "business revolution."

I'll show you things how I've created them, and I run my business differently from some of the other guys. This was why I felt I needed to write this book. You need to know it's possible for anyone to succeed. I went from starting with one machine, and I developed this side of the business to over 120 additional machines.

Like I did, you need to open your eyes and your mind to find a way out. You need to take a good look outside of any regular routine to see what's going on around you. Keep asking questions, gather information, and do some research. If you have tunnel vision, you'll become stuck in a rut.

If you do the same thing over and over again, you'll get the same result. That's like going to work, you do it over and over, and nothing will ever change. I choose to do my job; my way, with no boss looking over my shoulder. I choose not to become involved in work politics and all the drama which surrounds it. I decided on the bigger picture and looked for the ways to make it better. I chose to take control of my financial welfare.

I might do the things a lot of people might not do, because I chose to challenge myself every day. I put myself outside my comfort zone to learn. I wasn't a pro in any way; but merely driven to do better in finding solutions to problems. Truth be told, I'm not that good at selling!

If there's anything you learn from what I share, it should be:

The goal of this business isn't: "How much money can I make? But it should be: "How can I find solutions to my customers' problems and help find what they want?"

If you place your focus here and help find solutions for their problems, you can trust me that it works… because the money *will* come.

Anyone can start the same vending machine business, and they can buy the best machines and dot them around their vicinity. However, unless they know how to place their vending machines, and get customers to notice them in the vast sea of other vending operators, they won't stand a chance.

The secret to this business is about creating a niche for your operation. It's about offering customers the services which their current provider isn't.

Let's say a customer already has a vending provider who offers the same equipment with the same products at all at the same prices as you.

How much incentive is there to change to your service?

Absolutely zero!

But... you need to do something different and find people who need your help. When you focus on their needs and show them you are their solution to their problem, you can build a regular client base. Once you can do that, the vending business can provide you with lots of success.

2

How a Vending Service Operates

From my standpoint, I provide companies with the free use of vending machines (and coffee brewers), and in return, I place them within their companies. So, stocking machines with the product of their choice, and then returning on a regular basis to restock (and remove the takings from the machines, in the case of vending).

In a lot of cases, there's no contract to sign or obligation for either side, and as long as both parties are content, we can keep doing this business together.

It is our responsibility for machine delivery, and any repairs, maintenance or upgrades to the machines. In a nutshell, it is always the aim to make it easy for companies to do business. This makes it easy for them, because they aren't tied into any contract they are bound into.

All they need to do is make a decision: "When and where will we set up the machines?"

Getting Started

The one thing I see a lot of people doing is procrastinating, and seeing this makes me realize why they are stuck in their 9-5 daily grind. I've seen it and heard all the excuses for not doing something.

Your first step to start taking action and doing something toward the business, is to act, and not just keep talking about it. You need to make the commitment to get your business up and running.

As with the coffee brewers, there is still work involved, but it pays off. Each person has their own reasons for doing it, and mine was twofold: financial freedom and time freedom.

Locations

The hardest part I found (and much more than the coffee brewers side) was finding the right areas which *can* make money. With vending machines, there are no guarantees that people will by, but with the coffee brewers, there are a set number of employees who are drinking coffee. Vending can be a roll of the dice, and every location is different.

There are numerous factors you need to consider when setting up vending machines at a location:

- Number of employees who work there
- Number of days and hours of business
- Are there coffee trucks which visit the business?
- The salary range for the employees
- The age of the employees, younger people purchase from vending machines more than older people
- Are they asking you to pay a commission?
- Are there stores in the vicinity which sell similar products?

The hard part is; to determine which type of machines will suit their purposes, and also yours. It makes no sense setting up a soda, snack, and coffee vending machine in a company which employs less than 30 people.

Do this, and you'll quickly find you're throwing away sandwiches which expired because no one is buying, and gross sales would be less than $100. At this rate, it'd take years to pay off the equipment.

Let your customer know you will monitor sales before you set up other machines. It's better to always be honest with them. The secret to making this business profitable is in finding locations where you have steady sales. What you are making from the machine on a weekly basis is important here. This allows you to pay off your machines in the shortest possible timeframe.

What timeframe is reasonable? I personally aim for 12 months.

It is also crucial you're at the location and continuously making sure your machines never run empty. If you show and find the machines are empty, then you have a problem.

It might seem that if they are empty, there are high sales. This is true, but, you could be earning more. If the machine is empty, it means you've lost sales. This problem arises with big operators; they are continually running around trying to keep up with the restocking of their machines.

Remember what I mentioned earlier? It's all about finding a solution to your customers' problems. Don't let your machines become empty.

How to Determine a Good Location

People will tell you sports centers and recreational areas are great locations, while some say schools and big offices or factories are the go.

I've had factory locations which only employ 25 people, and these have sold (consistently) up to 8 cases of soda, plus around $100 in snacks.

On the flip side, I've had office locations with over 50 employees, and between both machines I've been lucky to reach $60.00 per week. This is why it's crucial to choose locations carefully, and not invest too much in a location to start with.

Smaller locations with a soda machine are a significant step, mostly because you can then determine the possibility of a snack machine if your drink sales are high enough.

Start Out Slow

There's no need to spend thousands of dollars on buying new machines for your locations right at the start, and there's no need to even have these machines in your possession to begin with.

All you need to know is where to locate your machines, which you'll then purchase, and how much they're going to cost (plus the delivery time). Unless you find a deal which is too hard to pass up, I don't see the point of having machines sitting in your garage which you've paid for.

In the beginning, decide which type of vending you want to get into. If you have coffee brewers on site, there is little point of a coffee vending machine. Do you want to take it step by step and build your business slowly? Or do you have the desire and capability to start off big and purchase a route with locations and machines already in operation? Both ways will require some learning curves and some financial obligations too. With these in mind, starting out slow is useful for learning the business, and to see how things work, as well.

If you decide on the other option and buy an existing route, ask the operator to train you, and to offer support (if needed) for at least the first six months. Customers become unhappy when their vending machine breaks down. If you can't fix it immediately, this can lead to more significant problems. Make sure this is factored into your budget.

3

Right Machines and Right Price

At this point, personal preference comes into play, and buying new or used machines depends on your decision for your business. I will tell you, new machines are costly, and if you're starting out and have a limited budget, these used machines will work in your favor.

New soda machines can cost from $2500-$6000, whereas a new snack machine can cost $3000-$5000. A used soda machine should range from $1000 (for a 10 to 15 year-old single priced machine) to $2000, for a more recent multi-price machine, which can vend a variety of beverages and various sizes.

Coffee machines, however, come with premium prices with newer models costing $5000-$10,000 for a single cup coffee machine. On the other side of the coin, a 10-15 year-old machine can be bought for around $1600-$2000.

New food machines fall in the mid-range of a new coffee machine, with used reaching up to $3500.

The primary vending machine manufacturers which I've found to be durable and reliable are:

Soda Machines - Dixie Narco, Vendo, and Royal Vendors.

Snack and Food Machines - Automatic Products, Rowe and National Vendors.

Coffee Machines - Avalon and National Vendors.

I always look for a dealer who provides good machines, a great warranty, and top-rated service for their machines. Be sure you can easily find and buy spare parts if you need them. If you have a problem, you'll need to fix it within 24-hours.

Getting Free Machines

One of the best ways to start in this business is by not needing to purchase some of your vending machines. The two biggest soda companies (Coca-Cola and Pepsi) have plenty of programs geared toward vending operators. Here they'll allow an operator the use of their machines free of charge.

In return, you are then required to buy a particular amount of soda from them over a set period of time. I've personally used this method for a good many years. The advantages of this are, of course, the free machines... and they cover all repairs and maintenance costs, which is awesome!

The disadvantages are a limited selection because you can only use Coke or Pepsi products. My recommendation is to start your business purchasing a few used machines and get them established, and then you can contact Coke or Pepsi after that time.

This way, you build credibility as an operator on your own merits, and not a new person in the industry who's taken the easy route, but I'll leave that decision up to you.

Machine Rentals

Another option I've used to test locations before spending money is to rent a vending machine. All you need is a rental company in your area who rent the machine out to you which you want, and then to site it and see how the sales perform after that.

In my area, there is a company who rents vending machines on a contract basis. They rent soda and snack vending machines (which makes it easy to test a location out).

Spotting Vending Opportunity Scams

You might've been to a seminar or trade show where companies give a presentation or sales pitch in an attempt to convince you: "Vending is all you'll ever need and want!"

These companies try to convince unsuspecting people to buy a bunch of overpriced vending machines without helping you enter into the business. Hence, this is another reason for writing this title.

You can find more reliable machines at lower prices, and like I said earlier, just look for reputable distributors in your area. It is also possible to find vending machine distributors on the internet. Go to Google and type in "vending machines." It really can be as simple as you make it.

4

How to Make Real Money in Vending

Now, even though we've been through the coffee brewers and where the profits are, in vending, for profit margins and sales, volume is the key here. I've found that soda and snacks offer the highest earnings of any machines in business.

Benefits of Owning a Soda or Snack Machine

Soda Machines:

- Soda comes with an extended expiration date, and many go as far as 8-9 months.
- They can cost around 35 cents, and you can sell it for up to $1.00 or more.
- Soda machines need minimal service and maintenance.
- Some machines sell bottled water, and at the cost of around 20 cents per bottle, profit is good.
- These machines can hold over 500 cans of soda, so this makes it easier to sell plenty of products, and with no need to repeatedly revisit your site.

Snack Machines:

- They can offer a variety of snack choices.
- The cost of the product is slightly higher, but you can also charge that little bit extra for these items.
- Chips cost about 40 cents per pack and sell for $1.00 or more.
- Chocolate costs about 60 cents per bar. I sell them for $1.25 each.
- Cookies, gum, and candy cost in the range of 50 to 70 cents each, and I can sell these for $1.25 or more, per pack.

Snack machines also have little maintenance and are reliable working machines. Out of all the things that have gone wrong with my snack machines, I've only fixed small things like:

- Replacing light bulbs
- Having the coin mechanism repaired
- Replacing the vend motor
- Replacing a PCB on a machine (once in 6 years)

Note: It's always handy to have a spare coin mechanism. It saves time, and your customers appreciate the prompt attention in fixing their machine.

Paying Machines off Quickly

Apart from getting free machines from Coke or Pepsi, paying off your machines is a vital part (and step) in the success or failure of your business. The most significant factor to paying off a machine as quickly as possible is actually dictated by the number of sales running through your machine.

When I set soda and snack machines at a location, the minimum weekly sales I look for are around $100, between both machines.

This is sensible because the cost to set up the location (usually) is around the following:

- Soda machine: FREE (Coke)

- Used snack machine: $2000.00
- Coins to add to the coin changer :$70.00
- Cost for the machine products: $150.00
- Machine moving expenses: $125.00

Total = $2275.00

At $100 per week, 50% of this is profit, minus taxes to the government. So it comes to around $50 per week, or $200 per month, or $2400 per year.

This formula means I can pay off my machine in one year. This is theoretical because some locations you set up will do better than (or worse than) others.

If you have locations which don't make high sales, it doesn't make any sense to keep your machines there. This is especially true if you have another place which requires you to purchase additional machines.

I give a few months of monitoring the sales volume, and then decide if I need to relocate the machine/s.

How to Get Your Sites to Pay for Your Products

Some companies might offer to pay a proportion of the cost of a can of soda or snack. This is to give their staff the chance of having drinks and snacks at a lower price. This can be so good for vending companies.

These subsidies might range from 25 to 50% of the cost per item, and in some rare instances, it might be the full 100% cost of the product price.

I also use this formula for an option for locations where sales volume is poor. Before I decide to pull the machines from the site, I give the company the opportunity of subsidizing a portion of the sales to keep the machines. In some other cases, I tell the company what the minimum sales requirements are to maintain a machine on their premises. Any shortfall, and they make up the difference on a monthly basis. More often than not, most companies won't pay a subsidy, but some will.

Picking the Right Machines for Your Locations

You will find some people want all types of machines for their location, and this might not be in your best interests. An office with around 30 employees might ask for soda, snacks, and food vending.

Food vending machines are expensive, and I wouldn't set one up at a location which had less than 200 employees.

I decide what machines can go at which locations like this:

1. **Less than 50 employees** – soda machine. Or a combination machine.
2. **50 to 75 employees** – soda machine and a small snack. Or a combination machine.
3. **75 to 125 employees** – soda and large snack machine.
4. **125 to 200 employees** – soda, large snack, and a coffee machine.
5. **200 and up** – soda, snack and food, and coffee, with bill changer.

This is my formula which I use in my business. It's up to you to determine what you're prepared to offer your customers. There is another factor to consider, and this is walk-thru traffic!

At some sites, it might be the walk-thru traffic which accounts for the more significant portion of your sales, so always keep this in mind.

5

How to Find and Buy Machines Cheaply

Other vending operators who are selling equipment can be a great way of getting cheap machines, and one way to find them is at the wholesalers or Cash n' Carry. Many have a display or even classified boards where various people can advertise for free.

You might find some great deals at a fraction of the cost compared to buying from a distributor. Do research first, and get an idea about what types of machines are selling for what price, by visiting machine sales companies.

Here is a link to a company which sells refurbished vending machines and spare parts: http://www.veii.com/

Getting Your Prospects to Call You First

This can be the most crucial step in the sales process, and getting potential customers to call you first is awesome. When they contact you first, they're looking to you as being the expert in your field, and you can help them with their problem, so be ready.

This can make your job easier, and it means you've gained more control too. It doesn't matter the method you use to do it, such as advertising, direct mail, or cold calling. The vital element is to provide them with your problem-solving information, and target them right at the crucial moment when their problem is hurting them the most.

I've found, over the years, there are a few common things which keep coming up, and I've taken their gripes and implemented solutions to them. When a company calls me to help, this is what I hear:

- Vending machines aren't restocked very often, and sometimes they're empty for weeks.
- If a machine breaks down, it's sometimes several days or even over a week for it to be fixed.
- The product selection is poor, and some products have expired or are very close to expiring.
- The products we ask for are never in the machines.
- The machines are old, and the products keep sticking.
- Healthy options are requested but we don't get them.

Understanding Customers to Keep Them Happy

Customers want to feel like they're important, so make sure you remember it was your customer who made the decision to give the business to you. For this reason, you need to make sure you honor your word and live up to what you promised, otherwise the connection will be lost, and quickly.

Keeping their machines clean and stocked is one thing which goes a long way to keeping customers happy. If they make any requests for new products, you should aim to accommodate them.

This will prevent you from becoming like all the rest, and I've found asking employees how they like the machines is one of the best ways of maintaining an excellent service.

Use the above information the best way you can to keep your accounts. Be sure to develop relationships with staff, over time. I don't come in every week and fill the machines without speaking to someone. I make an effort and make a connection by talking to people on a first name basis. Don't give your customer a reason to change their vending company. Be irreplaceable!

6

New Machines Versus Used, and the Difference of Prices

New machine prices vary depending on:

- Product holding capacity
- Amount of various selections
- Single priced items vs. multi-priced items
- Bottle vending or can vending machine
- Guaranteed vending capabilities

Other factors to consider:

New machines use different technology than old models, and some machines only use certain kinds of coin mechanisms. E.g. MDB coin mechanism.

New Soda Machines

- New soda machines will come with either flat front, bubble front, or glass front, and with 6 to 10 selections
- Most nowadays are multi-price machines
- Bottle drop glass front machines are very appealing and look great, but are expensive

- You might also need a coin mechanism or bill changer to accompany the machine
- New coin mechanisms cost around $375 to $425, and bill changers fall in the range of $400 to $500

New Snack Machines

New snack machines are priced on capacity and selection. A base snack machine model usually contains 4 chip trays, a tray for candy, and will hold around 240-300 items.

An average price will range from $3000 to $5000, depending on the model, and the number of trays and capacity, as well.

On some of the most recent snack machines, there is a thing called "Guaranteed Delivery" or "Sure Vend" technology. With this, the machine knows if the product has been dispensed into the receiving bucket.

If the product doesn't drop, the machine will automatically attempt another, and if this fails the machine automatically refunds the customer's money.

Used Snack Machines

The average price will range from anywhere between $1400-$3000, and is dependent upon the machine's age, model, the number of trays, and overall capacity. You can also put used bill changers and coin mechanisms in for these machines. Prices here range from $175-$300, depending on each changer.

I'd recommend starting out buying a used snack machine and giving it a fresh coat of paint and a good cleaning.

Combination Machines

New soda and snack combo machines come priced between $4000-$6000. If they can find a used one, then you should look to spend between $2400-$3400. A combo machine is excellent for a smaller location which might have limited space requirements.

New Coffee Machines

Prices can range between $4000, all the way up to $8000.

A lot depends on the model, the number of selections, and if it's a fresh brew or a bean grinder. You need to understand your location for this type of machine. You should also note: coffee machines require much more maintenance and cleaning to keep them running correctly.

Used Coffee Machines

Average price ranges of coffee machines are $1800-$3500, depending upon the model and the number of selections, plus the machine's age.

New Food Machines

Prices for these machines are very high, and be prepared to spend $6500-$8500, if not more.

Food machines are highly flexible for selling numerous types of products, ranging from sandwiches, salads, and beverages, including milk and some meal solutions too.

Used Food Machines

The prices range from $1800-$4000, depending upon the model, age, and the condition.

Another thing to note is food machines are more expensive to repair and maintain as they are highly sophisticated machines. As an example, changing a cold air compressor is about $1000 or more.

7

How to Keep Costs Down and Some Other Great Tips

You can reduce costs considerably when you take your time and do plenty of research. And, these used machines are an ideal way to start and keep capital costs down.

You can run this business from home. I still do, and began with using my car; loading soda and chips and chocolate bars on the rear seat and in the trunk.

Business Licensing Registration

There are various ways to set up your business.

- Sole Proprietorship
- Partnership
- Corporation

In the US, check this link and choose the type of business structure which suits your needs best:

http://www.sba.gov/smallbusinessplanner/start/chooseastructure/index.html

In Canada, to register your business name and get all the information you need about government regulations, these can be found here:

http://www.canadabusiness.ca/eng/page/2730/

In the UK, check this link to see which type of business suits your needs best:

http://www.businesslink.gov.uk/bdotg/action/layer?
topicId=1073858805&r.s=tl

Registering a business isn't a vital step in the beginning. But, it should be on your agenda for later. To begin, keep track of your purchases and expenses which you will incur while in business.

Keep track of sales and record them daily and also make sure to have a person who can do your income tax, and make a statement of business activities form, too. Check your locality for guidelines needed there.

Selling Machines or Locations

If you come to the decision to sell a location or any of your machines, you really need to decide which price seems worthwhile to you, and to your customer. Almost everyone I speak to in this business has their own perspective on what is the right way to calculate these values.

If I'm selling a machine, I look at the condition, age, and the value. If I'm selling a location, I calculate weekly gross sales which the site produces, plus any depreciated value of my machines.

If the machine takes $100 each week in sales, then I'm looking to 8 to 12 months profit as a price, if I can get it. That's around $2400 in profits, plus an amount for the goodwill of my machines.

Referrals

When you have good relations with customers, over time you can get referrals. I've found some employees change jobs and move to other companies. If their vending provider isn't up to scratch, I sometimes get the call for help!

To Pay or Not - Commission

Everyone always wants a piece of your pie; it might be the government or your customers. They'll all want a bit of it. With the government, the only way you have any control is when you write off expenses in your business. Check with an accountant on that one. Localities will differ in this regard.

If you offer a commission to a customer, you could find it isn't always needed. I don't, and I think my services and my offer to place machines which I spend thousands of dollars on is more than enough of a great gesture.

Some people ask: "How much will I get?"

I tell them I need $1.00 for chips and $1.25 for all the other items to run the business effectively. If they demand and wish to earn a commission, we need to raise the price of the products. I'll tell them honestly, if they are set on it.

I've had situations where I've offered commission, and the sales are much less than expected. I talk to the contact person that I dealt with and explain the situation.

This is how I'd say it:

"I just want to speak to you, and let you know how things are progressing with the vending machines. I've come to notice the sales aren't as expected. In fact, the sales are only … (the amount) per week, and I'm (unfortunately) not going to be unable to continue paying any commission because of the low sales volumes. Please understand I need to do what is best for my business as well as your customers and/or staff."

I've had a good response using this type of approach, and most respond well because it makes sense and you're being completely honest with them.

Transporting Your Machines

You should always make use of reliable moving companies to move your machines for you. Any delays (and I've had plenty) doesn't work well with this business. It's even worse when you give your customer an ETA (estimated time of arrival), and it doesn't happen. I use a reliable mover who has helped me on numerous occasions. You will find good movers charge $60 to $75 per hour, and you can expect to pay in the region of $75 to $200 for a basic move.

8

Office Coffee Businesses and How They Operate

When you decide to become an office coffee operator, the objective is to provide the free use of brewing equipment to numerous businesses. Yes... free of charge.

In return for this, all we ask of them is that the company purchases their products from us, and this would include such things as:

- Coffee
- Cups
- Lids
- Stir Sticks
- Creamer
- Milk
- Sugar

So then; what is required from us (the operator) is to visit the company each week, and then take a look at what items are needed for restock. From this point, we purchase the supplies and then pass on an invoice to the company when we deliver their items.

Simple, and straightforward! I like the simplicity here, don't you?

Many companies supply these items to employees at no charge, and this is where we can have a gained advantage and make a big profit. A lot of this is down to the fact that these companies don't have the time to go and purchase many of these items each time they are required, and it's much easier if they ask someone "like us" to do it for them.

How Much Can You Make?

This depends on which products you offer to your customers, and the volume they purchase from you.

As a rough working example, if you can find 10 places which will allow you to set up operation, and you make $50 per location, you've made $500 per week. In my eyes, that's a nice amount to make for not much work at all.

Even with the list of coffee supplies I've just mentioned, I personally offer a broader range to my customers. I've also branched out and supplied paper towels, soap, garbage bags, and other cleaning materials to some customers, and they appreciate this because it means their life becomes easier. I am offering them a solution, or in this case, solutions. They like it when their life becomes easier.

On the odd occasion, the request has been made to me to purchase items for their office, and have included kettles and toaster ovens, as examples. All of this will depend on the needs of your customers and in your willingness to buy these items on their behalf.

Personally, it makes a lot of sense to me, mostly because I go out anyway to purchase items for my business. One more stop on the way makes very little difference in time and effort required, and is negligible. There is also the fact you have an excellent chance to add to your business profit.

Here are examples of my purchases and my pass on prices which I've used in the past:

Case of coffee – Cost $30.00 – Retail – $50.00

Foam cups – Cost $22.00 – Retail $48.00

Sugar sachets – Cost $6.50 – Retail $15.00

Drinking chocolate – Cost $8.00 – Retail $14.50

Tea (Tetley) – Cost $7.50 – Retail $10.00

Sweetener – Cost $16.00 – Retail $23.00

Case of soda – Cost $8.00 – Retail $12.00

Bottled water – Cost $4.50 – Retail $10.00

Paper towels – Cost $12.50 – Retail $21.00

Dish soap – Cost $9.99 – Retail $15.00

This list could go on and on, but you should see my point here. This is only a few of the necessary items which I purchase for some locations, and there are many other products which I don't buy as regularly.

At this point, all I do is purchase the items and mark them up to what I think is reasonable, and then make out the invoice for the increased price and hand it to them. All of them pay within a couple of weeks, or whatever the payment terms are that we have set, so everyone is happy with this arrangement.

The best thing about it is, it isn't rocket science, and hardly takes much thought or effort to run. Most items are purchased at the local grocery stores or department stores where I then add the increase (to earn a decent profit). The invoice books can be purchased at any good stationers such as *Staples*, and that is basically all I do.

9

How to Do the "Office Coffee" Setup

The first thing is: to find a company which is selling coffee brewing equipment, and by this, I don't mean home models. Actually, these are purpose-built for offices or commercial areas.

One site which can give you some ideas is:

Bunn Thermal Brewers -
https://www.dccoffeeproducts.com/bunnthermalserver.html

You can also do a Google search and see which companies are selling these sorts of machines in your locality. All you need to search for is "thermal coffee brewers."

The model which I use for a lot of success is the *Ace D Series Automatic Coffee Brewer*. I think these are the best type you should aim for, because of the quality, or something very similar.

I choose these models because they have an extra faucet which dispenses water for the employees who wish to have tea or hot chocolate, as opposed to just coffee. I know what you're thinking, how much does a system like this cost?

New Units - $500 to $750, or higher, and this does depend on model and features given.

Refurbished and Used - $150 - $300.

You can also purchase thermal coffee canisters which hold coffee and keep it warm for hours, and these cost anywhere between $90 to $120, or upward, brand new.

Personally, I always buy new units. However, I've seen some excellent refurbished ones. The choice is up to you at the end of the day, because (I do know) it does sound like a great deal of money.

The point here is: you need to make some sort of investment to start a business and earn a profit. I studied this for a long time, and I know these coffee brewers fit in well with office environments, and that they are very robust.

With regard the thermal canisters, these are great for holding hot coffee and using in meetings which make them very flexible for my customers. As they are similar to a home thermos, they can be carried around by the handle and located anywhere (without the worry of burning any surfaces they are placed on).

With the equipment I supply, I always get great reviews because the coffee is still hot for hours after it's been brewed.

Here is an example of a delivery I make to one customer each week.

Coffee 2 cases x $50.00 = $100.00

Tea 2 boxes x $10.00 = $20.00

Chocolate 2 boxes x $14.50 = $29.00

Soda 1 case x $12.00 = $12.00

Water 1 case x $10.00 = $10.00

Paper Towels 3 bundles x $21.00 = $63.00

Total $234.00

My product purchase price = $141.00

Profit = $93.00

This isn't much under $100.00 profit for one week, and it's only for one customer after I've purchased all of the products they need. This is one of many accounts I hold, and the cost of the coffee brewer will be paid off in a couple of months, with an account such as this one.

This simple example shows there is money to be made, and it is straightforward; how you too can make this money. Apart from going to the cash and carry, and purchasing the desired products, the only work I perform is visiting the client for 15 or 20 minutes each week. Here I check the machine and see which items they require for the following week.

When I visit the customer, I'm not in and out as quickly as possible, though. I spend some time cleaning the coffee brewer and the surrounding area, as well. After that, I make sure all their supplies are topped up and ready to go.

So far, all of this is very simple, and I know you're probably asking: how can I find these accounts, and which locations should I check?

There is going to be some work to do up front, and no business can start without this work being done. The main things you need to do are: locate the best place to purchase your brewers, and then begin the hunt for your locations.

10

The 6 Methods I Always Use

There are six methods you can use in finding locations, and I use all of them. The oldest method in anyone's book is known as cold calling. Here, you knock on doors and meet businesses face to face, and from there; you need to pitch your proposal to them. This method is the most time-consuming. However, it still works, very well; I might add.

With this one, there is plenty of legwork involved, and you can be out for the best part of a day scouting for locations. I can advise that walking into a building and speaking to a receptionist at the front desk won't work, though. If that isn't enough, there are a fair share of buildings which have a sign up saying, "No Soliciting."

I generally (on most occasions) ignore the sign for one simple reason: it doesn't matter which area of business you're working in, it's all soliciting. You always sell yourself and what you are offering. Let's look at method one, now.

Method One: I circle the building I am considering approaching and I check how many cars are in the parking lot. This can be a great indicator of how many people work there.

Second to this, I attempt to enter through a rear entrance (if they have one). If it is a manufacturing operation, they might have a loading bay, and with this, I always seem to glean extra information from the workers on how they operate in the offices.

Questions you should ask in the cold calling method:

1. Does your company office use a coffee service here?
2. How many people are working here?
3. Do you know the name of the person who I'd speak to about placing a coffee brewer here?
4. Do you know if they're available to speak with me now?

I always ask these questions, and depending on the answers I receive, I can determine if the location has the potential of me placing a coffee brewer onsite. In case you have a chance to speak to a company representative or the person who make the decisions, be sure to have more information with you.

I personally have information on the brewer, with a picture attached of it. With this, I fasten my business card and a product list of the products I offer.

Although this is a time-consuming method, I've made many successful placements this way, and it is way cheaper than advertising.

One final note is to make sure you get the person's name who you spoke with, because you'll need to follow up. And if they offer their contact details, this can be a good sign you might be onto a successful placement. If you don't push for it, there's no one else who is going to do it for you.

Method Two: B2B Business Directories

You can find a B2B business directory in many areas, although, I found a trip to the public library is often one of the easiest. Many states will have their own. Then you'll know that all the businesses are local. You can purchase these directories, but it is better not to waste money and put it toward your first coffee brewer instead, because they can be expensive.

These B2B directories contain all the relevant information about all the companies in your area, including:

- Number of Employees
- Contact Names
- Annual Sales
- Business Description

I find these to be very useful in narrowing down my search and finding companies I wish to contact. When you have things like "employee numbers," you can see they've probably got the need for a coffee brewer, or more.

A lot of towns and cities also publish business directories, although these might not be as in-depth as a B2B directory. It doesn't matter which directory you use. Ultimately, you need to compile the information to help develop your strategy, for when you approach these companies.

US Companies can be located at this website: http://www.jig-saw.com/

Canadian companies can be found via this website: http://www.scottsinfo.com/scottshome/default.aspx

A quick search on Google can also help. Type in "business directories" and your area locality, and you should get results of more local directories.

Method Three: Direct Mail

Once you've used the business directory and pinpointed businesses which you wish to approach, you can do so by writing directly to the contact person involved.

I've found it to be one of my least favorable methods, though. However, it does work, and just because I'm not a huge fan, it doesn't mean you might not be. As with anything, there is a skill in how you contact these companies when using direct mail.

I've found simple works the best, and with this in mind, I found a very brief sales letter or postcard style of advertisement will work the best. The secret with any sales pitch is to make your reader "want" to keep reading.

To do this, you need what they call "a killer headline" or something which will catch their attention when they read it. I also found the best thing to write is a "benefit-driven, problem-solving" statement such as:

"Are you tired of lousy office coffee suppliers and that bland coffee taste? We provide the best service, affordable products, and fresh coffee!

We have a Brand New Coffee Brewer with your company's name on it, just call us today!

Check our "New Product List" available now!

Call: Your Name on (123) 123-1234

You can experiment with the words, nothing is fixed, and some work better in some areas than in others. It can be a very cheap way of making contact, and costs less than a dollar to make contact with each company. This wording would be changed to fit in with vending machines if you opt for that side of the business also.

I always found it doesn't bring in the most significant amount of customers. However, if you make contact at the right time, and they are having problems with a current supplier, you might be in with ease.

Using this method, you should see a small percentage of companies who give an affirmative reply, and the most important thing to remember is you don't need lots of locations to make money, just a few prime customers are all that is required to pay dividends.

Method Four: City Building Permits or Municipal Departments

This method can be one of the best ways of finding businesses which are yet to open, or that are in development. If you visit your local office, you can view reams of business permits which present you with information on the business location, building, and business type, among other things which are of great use.

You can then visit the location from the listing and present them with your flyer, price list, and business card, ready for when they are due to open.

Method Five: Phone Book Advertising Pages

We all know advertising helps businesses to attract customers, and we know it does cost money, and in some instances, it can require a lot. A simple advert can cost upward of $25.00 per month.

If you are seeking to do some block advertising, the cost will range between $150 and $400 per month. At the end of it, it all boils down to the amount of exposure you want to receive. In the past, I've found it difficult to put a number on how much I've gained from using telephone book advertising.

I always needed to ask customers where they found my information, just to be sure. Unless you have plenty of funds available for this kind of exposure, you're better off sticking with the first options which are cheaper, and it is easier to know the results you're getting, and from where.

Method Six: Internet Search Listings

We all know how much the internet has grown and become a part of our everyday lives. It still continues to grow, because many businesses have yet to make full use of the online experience.

This method does require you to have a website where your information can be accessed by customers in your area. Like other forms of advertising, there is an art in making this method work for you, and much of what is written on your direct mail flyer is the same for the internet. Attention-grabbing headlines are super-important.

All websites must have great information because they are great tools for selling to prospective customers, and it gives them alternative ways of contacting you for information.

Most important; is a strong message and specific "calls to action" which encourages them to contact you. The internet really is a great tool where you are able to pitch your services.

I always go to a location to speak to the person concerned, because I like this way the most. I still go armed with a good quality picture of the brewer and the specifications, including my current price list and a business card. With all this in hand, they can see (there and then) what I'm all about, and how my products compare.

I provide free delivery and setup of the brewer in their location of choice, and I run through all the benefits of having this brewer on site, and how their staff will respond favorably to having it in place.

11

The Benefits of a Coffee Brewer and How to Set One Up

- They are ideal for serving fresh coffee in a waiting room
- Fantastic for meetings and functions
- You can easily transport the thermal brewer
- Staff appreciate fresh coffee which is company-provided

Things to consider:

- The product range you can offer can be endless once you find the customers who require your help
- Do you think there are companies out there who do need the help of a service such as yours?
- Do you think you can save companies money on their coffee bills, or any of your other products?

For a fact, I know some large suppliers who are overcharging their customers. You might be wondering how I know this, for sure. Well, it so happens; it's the first thing I ask a customer when they ask me for help.

"Can I take a look at their price list?" I'll ask.

From this, I can tell a customer which items they are being over-charged on. In most instances, these customers are more than happy to give me their competitor's price list.

When this is in my possession, I can see immediately where I can save them money, while at the same time making my percentage when they sign up with me. This being said, not all customers will make you privy to this information. After a time, though (and with more than one acquaintance), they might change their mind.

If you can get a price list early on, it is easy to make yours while coming in cheaper, and on the flip side, nothing is stopping you from creating your own and testing the waters with your prices. All you need to do is mark up your bought products by up to 30% and see what the response is.

All it takes is a few questions regarding your prices to find if they are appealing or not, then it's a matter of honing and fine-tuning your price list, until you know you can save any customer money.

The people you make contact with won't be the business owners, in most cases. They will be the person lower down who has had this task delegated to them, so be natural and be yourself, without appearing to be overly pushy.

Honesty in what you are aiming to achieve can work far better than attempting to "fool" a customer by coming across as cheesy or like a salesperson. I always explain I clean the equipment on a regular basis to make sure it is operating like it should be. This (like everything else) is included in the price of the brewer. "Free!"

That is pretty much all there is to it, and if you don't think there are opportunities for making money, here is a straightforward scenario for you to sink your teeth into…

If you only found one new location each month, or even if you just managed to find four new sites over the next six months, let's see:

If you managed to earn $50 per week profit, well, this can be done with selling one case of coffee, sugar, milk, and creamer, and some tea, for example.

This profit would equate to $200 per month, for each location. You are already up to $800 per month profit (with four sites). That can make your home grocery bill and vehicle purchase much more manageable. See what I mean? Imagine having 10 or more locations? Do the sums and see.

How to Set Up Your Coffee Brewer

It's not tricky setting up your coffee brewer. First, you have 2 types of brewers.

1. Pourovers - This type is where you'll need to manually fill a holding container with water, and pour the correct amount of coffee into the brewer.

2. Automatic - With this model, the brewer is connected directly to a water pipe and automatically refills the brewer's reservoir, while it then brews the coffee into the thermos.

The pour over models are more straightforward to set up and run because you can place them anywhere there is an outlet, and then all you do is plug them in. The automatic models *do need* to be near a cold water pipe so you can connect directly to the water supply.

Connecting to the water pipe is simple, just go to a local hardware store and purchase a "self-tapping valve," these should be a ¼ inch. All this is; is a valve which has a small needle at the end. When you place this against the copper water pipe and tighten, it slowly pierces the water pipe and connects the supply to your coffee brewer.

The valve comes with instructions and it's very easy to understand. Then you attach a plastic water pipe with the threaded nut to the "self-piercing valve," and the other threaded nut to your brewer.

Once your brewer is connected and running, it's merely a matter of hitting the *brew* button.

Once the Brewer Has Been Set Up

Once your brewer is connected, all you do is the following:

1. Turn on the water supply.

2. Turn on the brewer. There might be an on and off switch on the rear (as well as on the front).

3. Let the reservoir fill up with water and reach the correct brew temperature. Your machine might have a "ready to brew" light on the front.

4. When the brewer is ready, insert your coffee filter and add a packet of pre-packed coffee (which should be 2 oz -2.25 oz packets).

5. Push the *brew* button and then wait for the thermos to fill.

6. Pour a coffee by holding your cup under the thermos and pushing the button.

This is a basic and simple system. When you go out to look at brewers, ask the salesman to show you a brewer which is working and plumbed in. Tell them you're new to the industry and need some direction and instruction on how to set up the brewer. Any decent distributor should offer their help, especially if they want the sale.

12

Buying Supplies and Money Makers

There are several options for purchasing your products, and you should find a wholesale "cash and carry" in your area. The coffee you should buy is pre-packed coffee and comes in different weights. I use 2 oz. to 2.25 oz. packs of 100% Colombian, and I recommend the same.

You should check different locations to find the best prices. One thing I used to do was to visit each wholesaler and create a product list for my customers.

Tip: always, always be open with your customers.

I've had some customers tell me other companies wanted their business, but they wouldn't give them great prices. When I arrived and offered the entire package at no cost (and handed them a price list right there) they jumped at my offer!

What Products Earn You The Most Money?

Coffee is where you can make high profits, and if you sell a good coffee which people really like, it'll keep paying, week after week.

You can buy cases of coffee from $25.00 - $35.00 and then mark it up and sell it for $45.00 - $60.00. Companies pay this because this coffee is already pre-packed and serves between 8 or 10 oz. cups of fresh coffee, per brewing. Each coffee case can brew up to 60 pots of coffee.

Other products which have high-profit margins are your sugar, cream, hot chocolate, paper towels, paper plates, and more.

The key isn't making a massive profit from each item, but, because you mark up each piece and sell high volume, you'll make a significant profit.

Earning Customers' Trust

Here is where things get really good! When you've got a customer who you've developed a relationship with over time, that's when you'll have a customer for life. By delivering excellent service and keeping your promise of providing their products on time, and adequately running your business, professionally… your customers *will* stick around.

Understand it's not all about the products. It's more about you and your service. That is what is going to make people want to do business with you in the long-term.

I've had some of my contact people at my locations go on to different employment. And because I've developed a good relationship with them over time, I've found that many of them have called me (asking for my help) at their new place of business. I get this all the time, and I appreciate it, and so do they!

In Conclusion

Thanks so much for sharing your precious time here with me. I've now given you all the information on the coffee brewers and the vending side of my business, so you can see if it's a venture that you might like to explore for you. Now it's down to you on how you wish to proceed. I'd like to think you're not going to procrastinate, and instead, get moving with your business, regardless of which option you choose to take.

If you wish to start off small, you can use the coffee brewers to get footholds into companies first, and then see how they pan out for vending machines, later on. In many instances, even if you get rejected, you have contact details where you can make another proposal later on. Don't give up; to me it was never an option. And although (at times) I got frustrated, it was usually before something brilliant was about to occur, like a great machine for an awesome price, or new customers contacting me for my services.

I genuinely hope you'll go out and start your "office coffee" or vending business, and make the high profits you deserve to earn. If you use the steps I've shown in this book, and find a few awesome locations, you're well on your way to becoming a winner. You will begin seeing results! I have the utmost faith in you.

"Welcome to the world of coffee and vending machines… with a bit of candy, some chips, and even a hot chocolate or two to celebrate!"

I wish you so much luck and all of my kindest thoughts for your success, both now, and in the future.

Warm regards always, *James Moore.*

Made in the USA
Columbia, SC
05 July 2020